# Understanding
# St. John's Wort

FIRST

# Contents

# 1

# Introducing
## St. John's Wort

**S**t. John's Wort is one of the most successful natural medicines of recent times.

There is a significant body of scientific research supporting its use for treating mild to moderate levels of depression, and the widespread prevalence of this condition has meant that this beautiful, yellow-flowered plant is in high demand.

In 1998, sales of St. John's Wort in the USA totalled around $200 million, a figure that was substantially exceeded in Europe where total sales for 1999 were in the region of an extraordinary $6 billion.

Much of the popularity of St. John's Wort has been as a self-help remedy bought from pharmacies and health-food shops, but it is also prescribed by doctors in Germany, where, in the 1990s, it was given for around a quarter of all cases of depression seen by German GPs.

This level of use makes St. John's Wort not just one of the best-selling natural medicines, but one of the most widely consumed of all medicines.

## PRESCRIPTION DEBATE

Alongside the popularity of St. John's Wort, however, there has also been controversy. Despite being a herb with proven effectiveness and an excellent safety profile, there is still debate over how St. John's Wort works, which constituents make it work, how it should be taken, and when it should and should not be taken.

Perhaps the most potent example of the concerns that some have about St. John's Wort is that of the Irish Medicines Board (IMB), which decided to make the herb a prescription-only medicine in January 2000. This means that it can only be prescribed by a medical doctor, is not available in shops, and cannot be prescribed by natural therapists, including herbal practitioners.

The reason for the IMB's decision was partly that it considered that "patients with mild to moderate depression should be under medical supervision and that self-diagnosis and self-medication (non-prescription sale) are inappropriate." The IMB felt that people suffering from depression might choose to take St. John's Wort rather than see their doctor, and, consequently, these people might miss out on more appropriate and more effective forms of treatment.

To most authorities on the subject, the Irish decision is considered to be a huge and misguided overreaction; certainly no other European country has followed their lead. It is true to say, however, that St. John's Wort is ineffective for those suffering from severe depression, and that in such cases a medical practitioner should be consulted for advice and treatment.

The issue of when it is okay to take St. John's Wort yourself and when you should see your herbal practitioner, or doctor, is one of the topics covered in this book. We will also look at the other controversial aspects surrounding this marvellous herb. Drawing on the latest research and clinical experience, we will separate the facts from myth and misinterpretation.

# 2 A Brief History

**S**t. John's Wort is both an ancient remedy and a modern medicine.

It is mentioned in the earliest annals, including those of Dioscorides, Pliny and Galen, as well as most of the leading medical journals of today.

We know that it was used by several native American tribes to treat a range of conditions. The Cherokee used it for bloody diarrhoea (dysentery), externally on sores, as an infusion for fevers, applied externally for nosebleeds, as a poultice for snake bites, and as a wash to give strength to infants. The Iroquois also used it for fevers, and the Montagnais used it as a cough medicine.

WHAT'S IN A NAME?
Let's begin by looking at St. John's Wort's name, or rather names. Each plant has two kinds of name – a common name and a scientific one. A plant may have several common names, varying between different regions and countries, but it has only one scientific name.

Several different plants may have the same common name.

For example, there are many different 'fever trees' and at least five separate plants are known as 'Balm of Gilead'. To avoid confusion, botanists, horticulturalists and herbalists refer to plants mainly by their scientific names. The scientific name of St. John's Wort is *Hypericum perforatum*.

## THE BAPTIST'S PLANT

The latter part of the common name is most easily explained. 'Wort' is an Anglo Saxon word meaning 'plant', so this is 'St. John's plant'. The reference to St. John is to John the Baptist, and is connected with the time of year at which St. John's Wort comes into flower in much of Europe – around St. John's Day, June 24.

There is another likely association, which is that between the decapitation of John the Baptist and the traditional use of St. John's Wort as a wound-healing herb. Also, when the plant is crushed between the fingers, it tints them red and turns water, alcohol and oil red when infused in them – like blood.

The Feast of St. John the Baptist is actually the Christianisation of the summer solstice, midsummer's day, when Piedmont and Lombardy go out to search the oak leaves for the 'oil of St. John'".

He speculates about the

*On St. John's morning peasants of Piedmont and Lombardy go out to search for the oil of St. John*

the sun is at its highest point in the sky. In his celebrated work *The Golden Bough: A Study in Magic and Religion*, J.G. Frazer writes: "on St. John's morning (midsummer morning) peasants of origins of this oil and is clearly unaware of St. John's Wort. The oak does not produce any oil, but it may be that St. John's Wort oil itself was placed in the trees as part of a midsummer

11

ritual, since the oak is also a revered plant.

The fact that St. John's Wort has bright, sun-like flowers that open around the solstice would further have strengthened its own reputation as a sacred herb, in addition to its 'blood'-producing properties.

We know that it was viewed as a magical sun herb and was thrown on to midsummer bonfires, perhaps to celebrate the sun at its apex, and to plea for enough warmth and daylight to bring the crops to fruition before winter came.

## SCIENTIFIC NAME

The scientific – or botanical – name, *Hypericum perforatum,* tells us more about the nature of this plant and its traditional roles. 'Hypericum' derives from the Greek 'hyper', meaning 'over', and 'eikon', meaning 'icon'.

This relates to the practice of placing bunches of St. John's Wort over images, pictures or statues (icons) for protection and to ward off evil influences. The icon may have been a religious one or may perhaps have been an image of a loved one in need of care. It is possible that this practice was used to seek healing for the ill.

'Hypericum' is sometimes translated more generally as meaning 'to overcome an apparition', that is 'to ward off evil spirits'.

'Perforatum' is used to describe the appearance of the leaves of the plant when they are held up to the light. They are covered in translucent dots that look like perforations –

little puncture holes. These are actually oil glands, which, when crushed or placed in alcohol, oil, or hot water, release a red pigment – the 'blood' described earlier.

This red colour is formed by chemical compounds called 'hypericins'; these constituents were considered to be the main medically-active constituents in St. John's Wort until recently, but more of that in a moment.

# 3 What Is St. John's Wort?

**S**o what, exactly, is this herb with such an amazing history revealed in its names?

It is not a rare, exotic plant found in the depths of the rainforest, but a very common plant that is actually considered to be a troublesome weed in some of the areas where it grows.

St. John's Wort is a native British plant and grows in woods, hedgerows and grassland, as well as in disturbed or waste ground. It is also a native of Europe (apart from the far north), and of temperate Asia and North Africa. It has been introduced into western North America, where it has become naturalised and is known as 'klamath weed'.

FLOWER IDENTIFICATION

To describe its appearance, St. John's Wort is a smooth, hairless plant, growing to a height of between 10-100cm (4-40in). The stem is stiff and erect, and often woody at the base, and there are two raised lines running vertically along it. The leaves are dotted with translucent glands, and the flowers are a vivid yellow with five petals in a star shape and a central sprig of yellow stamens. Overall, it is a very attractive plant when in flower.

## WORTS AND ALL

St. John's Wort is a member of the *Hypericaceae* plant family, which includes about 370 *Hypericum* species. Several of these species closely resemble St. John's Wort in appearance, so it is important to know what you are doing if you collect this plant to ensure you get the right one.

Before moving on, let's look at some of St. John's Wort's interesting relatives. St. John's Wort is sometimes called 'perforate St. John's Wort' to distinguish it from other similar native species, such as:

• **Hypericum androsaemum** – this has a common name of 'tutsan'. It derives from the French 'toute-saine', which is translated as 'all heal', revealing that this species was also used medicinally. This plant occurs in the wild in the UK, and is widely grown as an impressive ornamental. It is a bushy plant, much larger than St. John's Wort, and possessing quite different and larger leaves, but a similar flower.

• **Hypericum maculatum** – this is called 'imperforate St. John's Wort' and has black dots rather than translucent ones.

• **Hypericum undulatum** – known as 'wavy St. John's Wort' on account of the wavy edge to its leaves.

• **Hypericum pulchrum** –referred to as 'slender St. John's Wort' since it is a particularly slender, graceful and elegant type of St. John's Wort.

• **Hypericum hirsutum** – this is 'hairy St. John's Wort', so named because it is a downy plant, unlike the smooth *Hypericum perforatum*.

Several species of Hypericum occur outside of the UK including:

• The Rose of Sharon, which is not, in fact, a rose but another *Hypericum* species, originating from the Mediterranean (*Hypericum calycinum*). Again, it is a large, bushy plant grown as an ornamental.

• Several North American

species are used by native American tribes. For example, *Hypericum ascyron* (known commonly as 'Great St. John's Wort') was used by the Menominee for kidney problems, weak lungs and tuberculosis, and by the Meskwaki as a snakebite remedy.

• *Hypericum aethiopicum* is a native African species. The roots were used in enemas for backache, and loin pain due to kidney or abdominal problems, and otherwise for fevers, wounds, sores, ear complaints, and sexually transmitted infections. This plant is known by several names by the Zulu including 'isimonyo'.

## CONSERVATION STATUS

In terms of conservation, St. John's Wort is very healthy. It is prolific in the wild to the extent that, in some parts of Africa, Australia and North America, it is considered to be something of a pest. Because it grows easily, it can be readily cultivated for medicinal use, so there is no need to harvest it from the wild.

The yield of leaves and

flowers, which are the parts of the plant used medicinally, is also good since the same plant can be cut two or three times each year. Although it is important to point out that the natural woodland habitats in which St. John's Wort grows need to be protected and preserved, the lack of conservation concerns about the plant itself is a real advantage. Other currently popular herbs, such as some echinacea species (e.g. *Echinacea angustifolia*) and golden seal (*Hydrastis canadensis*), have become endangered in the wild due to medicinal demand.

## CHEMICAL CONSTITUENTS

The main chemical constituents in St. John's Wort are:

- Naphthodianthrones – e.g. hypericin, pseudohypericin
- Phloroglucinols – e.g. hyperforin
- Flavonoids – e.g. quercetin, hyperoside
- Proanthocyanidins – e.g. catechin

- Volatile oil (essential oil).

*HYPERICIN AND PSEUDOHYPERICIN*

These are known as 'total hypericin' or 'hypericins'. The hypericins were long thought to be the most significant of the plant chemicals (phytochemicals) in St. John's Wort. Many of the clinical trials and other research projects into St. John's Wort have involved either purified isolated hypericins or preparations of the whole plant that have contained a specific amount of hypericins (i.e. they have been 'standardised' for total hypericin content).

*HYPERFORIN*

More recent studies, however, have shown that hyperforin is more strongly associated with the antidepressant activity of St. John's Wort.

Many of the tablet or capsule preparations available on the market are standardised for hypericins and guarantee a certain hypericin content. However, some newer products are standardised for hyperforin instead.

## FLAVONOIDS AND PROANTHOCYANIDINS

These have antioxidant properties, protecting the body's cells and helping to prevent heart disease and some cancers.

As with most medicinal plants, it is probably the combination of the various constituents that works best rather than one individual ingredient. For this reason, herbal practitioners usually prefer to use the whole plant, without it being manipulated to contain more or less of any one given chemical.

It is possible to check the quality of herbal preparations and ensure that there are the right amounts of a broad spectrum of the desirable chemicals present in the product without artificially altering their relative amounts.

Most herbalists would rather use a St. John's Wort preparation that has a natural balance of constituents, achieved through good growing, harvesting and processing, over one that has unnaturally high amounts of one element, as in many standardised products.

# 4 How Does It Work?

**I**n common with many medicinal plants, the exact ways in which St. John's Wort achieves its wide range of actions are not entirely understood.

Since medicinal plants contain several hundred chemicals, it can be hard to say which chemical does what, and how the plant interacts with the body.

It is a common misunderstanding to assume that herbal medicines are very simple medicines – in fact, the opposite is true. Herbal remedies are much more complex and difficult to understand than the comparatively simple structures of conventional drugs.

We do know, however, that St. John's Wort influences the nervous system in exerting its effects on our mood. To understand what St. John's Wort does exactly, we need first to have a basic understanding of the special chemicals (called neurotransmitters) that are involved in nervous system functions.

## NERVE NETWORK

Nerve cells conduct messages by

passing neurotransmitters between the ends of their individual cells. Chemically, these neurotransmitters are in the amine group, which includes serotonin, dopamine and noradrenaline. We need an adequate number of these neurotransmitters for the nervous system to be able to maintain our mood on an even, contented, keel.

## TAKING ACTION

In depression, the amounts of these feel-good chemicals decrease and this is associated with the symptoms of depression, such as lack of motivation, lack of interest in life, poor appetite, and sleep problems. If we can increase the amounts of serotonin, dopamine and noradrenaline, or prolong the time that they remain exerting their effects between the nerve endings, then our mood will improve.

One effective way of doing the latter is to prevent these neurotransmitters from being reabsorbed back into the nerve cell that they came from, meaning that they remain doing their job for longer, and therefore enhance our mood more substantially. Conventional antidepressant drugs, such as Prozac® and Seroxat®, do this with serotonin and are known as selective serotonin reuptake inhibitors (SSRIs).

St. John's Wort appears to have similar effects on serotonin, extending the time that it is available to improve the performance of the nervous system in terms of our feelings of positivity and wellbeing. Whole St. John's Wort preparations, and isolated hyperforin, appear to cause this effect.

Another way of improving the lifespan of amine neuro-transmitters is to disable the enzyme that normally breaks them down. The enzyme is called monoamine oxidase, and drugs that disable it are called monoamine oxidase inhibitors (MAOIs).

MAOI ACTIVITY

A possible, very slight MAOI activity for St. John's Wort has been suggested in some research studies, but the effect is so weak that it is probably not actually

# THE NERVE NETWORK

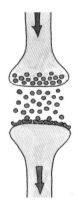

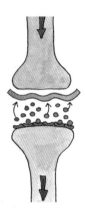

*Seratonin travels from the pre-synaptic nerve to receptors on the post-synaptic nerve in the direction of the nerve impulse.*

*Normally, the seratonin returns to the original nerve to be broken down. Note: MAOIs prevent the breakdown of seratonin so it can be secreted again.*

*With St. John's Wort, seratonin is inhibited from returning to the original nerve. Therefore it remains to continue stimulating the connecting nerve.*

involved in the antidepressant action of the herb.

This is an important point, since people taking MAOI drugs need to avoid eating foods containing the amine tyramine (such as Chianti, yeast extracts, cheese, pickled herring, and fermented soya bean products) otherwise their levels of amines can rise too high and cause problems.

This usually takes the form of a dangerous rise in blood pressure accompanied by a throbbing headache. A number of articles and books have given inaccurate advice stating that people taking St. John's Wort need to avoid tyramine foods. This is not the case, since the plant's effects on monoamine oxidase are so weak. In fact, no cases of interactions between tyramine and St. John's Wort have been reported.

# 5

# Drug Research

**S**t. John's Wort is one of the most heavily researched of all herbal medicines.

There have been more than 35 trials into its use as an antidepressant, which meet the highest research standards.

In these, it has shown similar effectiveness in relieving mild to moderate degrees of depression as commonly used conventional antidepressant drugs – for example: imipramine (Tofranil®), Prozac® and Lustral® – but with far fewer side-effects. Some of these studies have been criticised because they have looked at only small groups of people or they have been very short-term, often looking at only six to eight weeks of treatment with St. John's Wort.

Many herbalists believe that treatment needs to extend over eight to twelve weeks to build up maximum effects. However, it is interesting to examine the results of some of the more significant trials.

ON TRIAL

Two trials have suggested that

St. John's Wort may be as good as light therapy in treating seasonal affective disorder (SAD), the type of depression linked to lack of sunlight in the colder months.

A major research study disputes the usefulness of St. John's Wort in helping people suffering from depression. This study cost around $4 million,

◀ Research is proving the value of St. John's Wort.

and was funded by the National Center for Complementary and Alternative Medicine of the American National Institutes of Health.

The research findings were published in the *Journal of the American Medical Association* in 2002, and showed that St. John's Wort was ineffective in treating people experiencing severe levels of depression.

However, this study merely proved what herbalists already knew: that St. John's Wort is an excellent remedy for people with mild to moderate levels of depression, but is not strong enough to significantly assist those who have very pronounced forms of depression.

In fact, very few drugs can help in such cases. The study in question also looked at the effectiveness of the SSRI drug Lustral® for severe depression, and found that it too failed to be of help.

People with severe depression are unable to carry out everyday work and family commitments, they cannot conduct any semblance of a normal life, and may be suicidal. Such people need intensive support, counselling and psychotherapy in addition to medication, if there is to be any chance of making progress.

## STUDY SUCCESSES
A number of studies have monitored the effect of St. John's Wort in the treatment of specific conditions and diseases.

### THE MENOPAUSE
A large trial involving 812 menopausal women looked at how their symptoms responded to taking a mixture of St. John's Wort and the North American herb black cohosh (*Cimicifuga racemosa*).

The results showed improvements for symptoms such as poor concentration, and hot flushes.

### COLD SORES
The St. John's Wort pigments hypericin and pseudohypericin have been shown to attack several viruses known as 'enveloped viruses'. These include the herpes virus that causes cold sores.

## FIGHTING AIDS

Several small studies have shown moderate effects against retroviruses – the type of virus that causes AIDS. Research looking at purified hypericin, often given by injection, has demonstrated rises in the immune cells that are sensitive to the AIDS virus (CD4 T-cell counts). Although it is unclear how such research might relate to taking whole herbal preparations of St. John's Wort by mouth, the herb has been popular with AIDS patients and those who are HIV positive for several years now. There is a concern here, though, since St. John's Wort can affect the potency of some conventional anti-HIV drugs.

## SKIN CANCER

Experiments have shown promise for isolated hypericin combined with laser-light treatment in treating skin cancer. The hypericin is injected into skin tumours and then the tumour is subjected to laser light. Of course, this is very much a non-herbal use of St. John's Wort.

# 6

# When To Use
# St. John's Wort

**A**lthough best known today as an anti-depressant, St. John's Wort can help to treat many other conditions.

In 1998, a survey of members of the National Institute of Medical Herbalists showed that they were using it for the following conditions:

- Anxiety
- Depression
- Digestive problems
- General and trigeminal (facial) neuralgia
- Immune support
- Insomnia
- ME and chronic fatigue syndrome
- Menopausal problems
- Multiple sclerosis
- Pre-menstrual syndrome and other gynaecological problems
- Rheumatism
- Shingles
- Traumatic nerve damage
- Urinary problems
- Viral infections
- Wound healing.

## NERVOUS SYSTEM

St. John's Wort can strengthen the nervous system; it is

uplifting and promotes emotional stability. It is a nerve tonic, and can be used whenever the nervous system is under sustained pressure, such as during periods of stress, whether at work or at home.

If you are feeling emotionally or mentally strained, St. John's Wort can help to protect the nerves. It is known as a nervous system 'trophorestorative', meaning that it can help to restore normal balance and resilience to the nerves. Because of this, it is of value whenever you are feeling

▲ Dried St. John's Wort: This is one of the most versatile of the medicinal herbs.

depleted, fatigued, exhausted, and simply worn out.

As a herb that is healing, nourishing and nurturing for the nervous system, it makes an excellent convalescent herb when recovering from illness, especially viral infections.

It is also useful following emotional trauma, such as bereavement or as a result of family problems or relationship break-ups, which, in themselves, can cause depression.

As we have said earlier, St. John's Wort is suitable for treating many cases of mild to moderate depression, but not severe depression. It is especially useful for people who do not tolerate conventional antidepressant drugs, or for those who would rather try a gentle herbal medicine, with very few side-effects, before moving on to a stronger drug if it proves to be needed.

St. John's Wort also has a role to play in helping anorexia nervosa, excitability states (including hyperactivity and attention deficit hyperactivity disorder – ADHD), anxiety, melancholy, seasonal affective disorder (SAD), and insomnia. In some of these conditions, additional help will be needed, such as counselling in anorexia and nutritional corrections in

▲ *St. John's Wort oil (left) and St. John's Wort tincture (right).*

ADHD. It is important to take a sensible approach to nervous system problems, seeking appropriate medical and psychological support in addition to considering using St. John's Wort. Herbal practitioners often use St. John's Wort in controlling the symptoms of multiple sclerosis, but this is an area for professional use only.

*PLANT PREPARATIONS*

For all the above indications, St. John's Wort may be taken as a tea, tincture, juice, or capsule. The oil applied externally can help to reduce the pain of neuralgia and sciatica. Internal preparations can be of value in rheumatism, muscle pains, and fibromyalgia (muscle tenderness and weakness).

## DIGESTIVE SYSTEM

St. John's Wort tea has long been used to stop diarrhoea because it has a binding effect on the bowel. The tea may also help relieve indigestion and worm infestations.

St. John's Wort oil is taken to calm stomach irritation (gastritis), stomach and duodenal ulcers, and for diverticulitis (when part of the bowel becomes lax and forms a small pouch that then becomes inflamed and painful).

It may also assist in healing small areas of bleeding in the stomach or bowels, but remember that if you ever see any blood in your motions, you should always discuss this with your doctor.

Because of its calming, astringent and healing properties, St. John's Wort tea may be of some benefit for those suffering from the inflammatory bowel diseases, Crohn's disease, or ulcerative colitis, although this is an area for professional treatment.

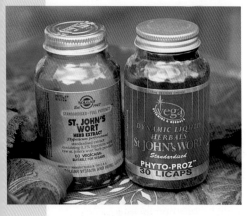

◀ St. John's Wort can also be taken in capsule form.

coughing up blood. It can be used today as a tea to soothe irritable coughs.

## SKIN

St. John's Wort oil can be used as a soothing and healing treatment applied directly to superficial burns (where the skin has not been opened), including sunburn.

If you do become sunburned, gently coat the burnt skin with the oil, and leave it on overnight

## RESPIRATORY SYSTEM

St. John's Wort was formerly used to treat serious lung conditions, such as tuberculosis and for symptoms such as (cover your pillow or bed with an old towel to prevent staining). If you have caught the situation quickly enough (i.e. applied it the same day), you will often wake up with the burn all but completely healed.

The oil can be used for small wounds, shallow cuts, and grazes. The juice (which can be bought commercially), tea, or oil of St. John's Wort can be applied over areas of itching, and to treat cold sores around the mouth, shingles, bruises, and bedsores.

Taken as a tea, tincture, juice, or capsule, it is sometimes successful in reducing facial flushing (the face 'going red') due to anxiety (nervousness, shyness).

## URINARY SYSTEM

Several authorities recommend St. John's Wort as a remedy for children's bedwetting (nocturnal enuresis), and the tea, juice or tincture may be helpful in some cases.

## INFECTIONS

St. John's Wort has been shown to be effective against

enveloped viruses, such as hepatitis viruses, cytomegalovirus (a virus that can cause a type of hepatitis and which particularly affects people with severely depleted immune systems, such as AIDS patients), and the viruses that cause cold sores, genital herpes, chickenpox, shingles, and glandular fever (infectious mononucleosis).

Some cases of ME/chronic fatigue syndrome have been associated with having a previous viral infection, such as glandular fever (Epstein Barr Virus), and St. John's Wort treatment may be helpful for such people.

## GYNAECOLOGY

St. John's Wort tea is helpful if you experience heavy blood flow during your periods, although the cause of this should also be sought with your healthcare professional. It is also helpful for premenstrual syndrome (PMS), especially what is known as PMS type D where the PMS is characterised by feeling withdrawn, depressed, tearful, forgetful, confused, and accompanied by sleep problems. St. John's Wort is also useful for mood changes around the menopause and for hot flushes.

## AGEING
As an antioxidant, St. John's Wort reduces damage to the body's cells, and may help to enhance longevity. Additionally, by reducing psychological stress and its impact on the body, this herb may also contribute towards easing the ageing process and keeping us looking

▲ *This amazing herb can even ease the ageing process.*

and feeling healthier for longer.

The tea can be taken as a regular beverage to promote these effects.

# 7 Possible Side-Effects

# St. John's Wort is considered to be a very safe herbal medicine.

The major concern is its potential to interact with conventional drugs; we will come to that in a moment. First, let us look at some of the possible side-effects of taking St. John's Wort.

- Dizziness
- Headaches
- Mild digestive upsets (such as diarrhoea and abdominal discomfort)
- Tiredness.

If you experience any of these symptoms, you should stop taking the herb – they will resolve once you do so.

If you notice these reactions, it may be that St. John's Wort doesn't suit you – at least at the particular time when you are taking it. Alternatively, there may be a problem with the type of preparation you are taking, or its dosage.

## LIGHT REACTIONS
Skin sensitivity reactions to light exposure while taking St. John's Wort have been recorded.

45

These 'photo-sensitivity reactions' are rare, but result in a skin rash. This is due to light interaction with the hypericins within St. John's Wort – pigments that respond to light.

It is wise for all of us to avoid excessive exposure to strong sunlight, but this caution applies particularly if you are taking St. John's Wort – especially if you are fair-skinned and therefore more susceptible to sunburn.

To avoid ultraviolet light exposure still further when taking St. John's Wort, it is important to avoid using sunbeds and tanning centres.

Again, concerns about the safety of artificial tanning using UV light means that it is wise for everyone to avoid these sources anyway.

## CATARACT CONTROVERSY

One study raised alarm regarding the potential for the development of cataracts (opacities in the lens of the eye) in St. John's Wort users. However, the research behind this has no relevance to human use of St. John's Wort and can be ignored.

The scare arose from experiments where pure hypericin was mixed in the laboratory with proteins from the lenses of calves' eyes and then exposed to light.

The result of these experiments was that the proteins from the calves' eyes formed into solid masses. This is the same sort of process that occurs in cataracts.

However, to suggest that there is any way that human eye lenses could become saturated with hypericin in this way, when taking St. John's Wort by mouth, is not only unscientific but patently nonsensical!

## PRUDENCE IN PREGNANCY

There is no evidence to suggest that St. John's Wort can cause harm to either mother or child during pregnancy, or when breastfeeding.

However, it is wise to avoid all medicines if possible during these times to reduce risks as much as possible, especially during the first three months of pregnancy.

## MIXING MEDICATION

With regard to interactions between St. John's Wort and conventional drugs, there are two areas of concern.

### ANTIDEPRESSANT DRUGS

The first is the potential for an adverse interaction with antidepressant drugs.

Because St. John's Wort influences the metabolism of neurotransmitters, including serotonin, there is a concern that it should not be taken at the same time as conventional antidepressant drugs that have similar effects. While low levels of serotonin are linked with depression, excessively high levels of this neurochemical can result in what is known as 'serotonin syndrome' where symptoms of confusion, fever, sweating, diarrhoea and muscle spasms are experienced.

Taking St. John's Wort at the same time as antidepressant drugs (especially the SSRI group, e.g. Prozac®) is therefore not recommended.

### NATURAL DETOXIFIER

The second area of concern

involves a larger number of drugs. St. John's Wort stimulates the activity of natural detoxifying substances (the cytochrome P450 enzyme system) in the liver.

This means that some of the drugs that are normally broken down by these detox enzymes may be broken down more quickly than would normally be expected. The end result is that the effectiveness of the drug is reduced.

The stimulation of the detox system by St. John's Wort is not in itself a problem. In fact, for people who are not taking the conventional drugs that are affected by St. John's Wort, this stimulation is a positively healthy thing – improving the rate at which waste products are removed from the body.

The problem arises when a patient's health depends on the drug that is being diminished by taking St. John's Wort.

Before we detail the types of drugs involved, it is crucial to be clear that it is not only St. John's Wort that has this stimulating detox effect on the liver.

Common foods, such as those

from the *Cruciferae* family (e.g. broccoli, Brussels sprouts, cabbage), red wine, and the pollutants called dioxins which are present in charcoal-grilled beef and cigarette smoke also cause this phenomenon.

*HARMFUL COMBINATIONS*

You should avoid taking St. John's Wort if you are taking any of the following drugs:

- **Anticoagulants**: blood-thinning drugs, especially warfarin
- **Antiepileptic drugs**: e.g. carbamazepine preparations (e.g. Tegretol®), phenobarbital, phenytoin preparations (e.g. Epanutin®)
- **Anti-HIV drugs:** such as the protease inhibitors (e.g. indinavir)
- **Cardiac glycosides**: the heart drug digoxin
- **Ciclosporin** (aka cyclosporin): this is a drug that suppresses the immune system and is taken by transplant patients
- **Contraceptive pill**: the suggestion that St. John's Wort might reduce the effectiveness

of the pill is still controversial. Some cases of breakthrough bleeding (menstrual bleeding outside of the expected time) have occurred when taking the pill and St. John's Wort together. This may indicate that the pill is not working properly and might therefore increase the risk of becoming pregnant. The risk appears to be small, however.

- **Theophylline**: used in some asthma drugs (e.g. Nuelin®).

It is also wise to stop taking St. John's Wort two weeks before undergoing a general anaesthetic. You should tell your doctor if you are thinking about taking St. John's Wort, particularly if you are taking a conventional drug on which your health depends.

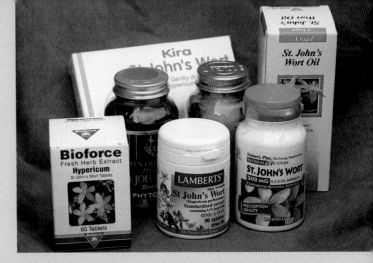

# 8 Using St. John's Wort

**S**t. John's Wort is used in a number of different types of preparation.

## TINCTURE

This is a liquid preparation made by extracting the dried or fresh herb in a water and alcohol solution.

The alcohol strength preferred is usually 45 per cent. The alcohol helps to extract and preserve the constituents in St. John's Wort.

Tinctures are made at varying strengths from 1:1 (one part herb to one part fluid), which is a stronger preparation, to 1:5 (one part herb to 5 parts fluid), which is a weaker preparation. I normally use the 1:2 or 1:3 strengths.

One study showed that the hyperforin content of fresh St. John's Wort tincture exceeded that of dried plant extract by 47 per cent; therefore, fresh tincture may be more effective than that made from the dried herb, especially for depression.

## TEA

St. John's Wort tea is made by infusing two teaspoons of the cut dried herb in hot water for five to ten minutes and then straining it before drinking. The tea has a rusty, orange-red colour and tastes dry, astringent and slightly sour; it is an acquired taste but is not unpleasant.

When buying loose dried St. John's Wort herb, you should check to see that the colour is a strong rusty-orange and is not faded, and that it smells fresh (and slightly fruity) not musty.

As well as being drunk, the tea can be used externally as a bath, compress, wash for open wounds, etc.

## OIL

St. John's Wort oil is made by gathering fresh flowers and then saturating these in enough cold-pressed, organic, extra-virgin olive oil just to cover them.

This oil/flower mix should then be exposed to sunlight, for instance on a sunny windowsill or ideally directly outdoors (bringing in at night), for two to six weeks until the oil turns bright red.

## JUICE

An organic St. John's Wort juice is available on the market and

can be used in similar ways to
the tea and tincture.

## CREAM
St. John's Wort cream is usually
made by infusing the fresh
flowers in a vegetable base
cream or adding the oil to a
base cream.

The cream can be used as a
general first-aid treatment for
small cuts, bruises, grazes, and
chapped lips.

A homoeopathic cream known
as 'Hypercal' is a combination of
homoeopathic potencies of St.
John's Wort (Hyper from the

▲ St. John's Wort oil changes colour
to red when it is exposed to sunlight.

botanical name *Hypericum*) and
marigold (cal from its botanical
name *Calendula*).

## TABLETS AND CAPSULES

Although these are very convenient preparations, they are not my preferred way of taking St. John's Wort. It is hard to compact adequate amounts of the herb into small tablets and capsules, and absorption may not be as good as for liquid preparations.

Additionally, most tablets and capsules available are standardised extracts, and I prefer to work with herbal preparations that do not contain exaggerated amounts of certain constituents (usually the hypericins) but instead offer a balanced range of the plants constituents at naturally

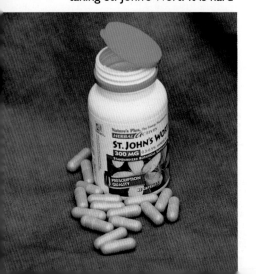

◀ Absorption of tablets and capsules may be inferior to liquid preparations.

occurring levels. In my own practice, I use traditional non-standardised preparations, such as the tea and tincture, in preference to tablets and capsules for my patients. Although tinctures are more convenient to use, I often find that the tea is the most effective way of taking St. John's Wort.

## GROW YOUR OWN

Whichever preparations you use, it is important to insist on organic cultivation of the herb. This means that your St. John's Wort preparation will not contain potentially harmful pesticide and herbicide residues. You can, of course, grow your own St. John's Wort supplies; it grows easily in full sun or slight shade on well-drained soil, and adds a vibrant dash of colour to the garden when in bloom.

Harvest the flowering tops, or the whole herb above ground (leaves, flowers and stems) just as the flowers are opening. You can then dry them for use as a tea, infuse them to make an oil, or even let them macerate in vodka for 14 days before straining in order to make a fresh tincture. (To do this, use 300g of freshly-chopped herbs to one litre of vodka.)

## HERBAL HARMONY

St. John's Wort combines well with other herbs for particular conditions. Herbal practitioners are trained to combine herbs so that they can act 'synergistically' together, meaning that the effects of the herb combination is greater than that of any single herb in the mix. My favourite St. John's Wort combinations are to couple it with skullcap (*Scutellaria lateriflora*) for anxiety states, and with oat straw (*Avena sativa*) as a restorative mixture for nervous depletion and fatigue.

## DOSAGE ADVICE

Dosages of the various St. John's Wort preparations vary depending on what you are using the plant for, e.g. higher doses are used for viral infections than for treating depression (see your herbal practitioner for guidance).

For general use as a mood enhancer and to protect the nervous system, the following doses are recommended:

- St. John's Wort tea can be taken at a dose of 2-5g per day, which equates to one to two cups made up with two teaspoons of the dried herb.
- The tincture (at a strength of 1:2) can be taken at a dose of 3ml once or twice a day.
- For capsules and tablets, a range from 500mg to 1800mg of standardised (for hypericins) St. John's Wort has been shown to be effective in clinical trials for mild to moderate depression. The commonly used standardised extract dose is 900mg per day (standardised for hypericins at 0.3 per cent) taken in three divided doses of 300mg each. Some newer standardised products are available based on 2-6 per cent hyperforin rather than hypericins.

TIME DELAY

The antidepressant effects of taking St. John's Wort typically take four to twelve weeks to build up, so you should allow this amount of time to elapse before deciding whether this herb is working well for you.

# 9 Resources

**HERBAL SUPPLIERS**

Gaia Garden Herbal Apothecary
2672 West Broadway, Vancouver
BC, Canada, V6K 2G3
www.gaiagarden.com

Penn Herbal Co.
10601 Decatur Road, Suite 2,
Philadelphia, PA 19154, USA
www.pennherbs.com

Napier's Direct
35 Hamilton Place, Edinburgh,
Scotland, EH3 5BA
www.napiers.net

Neal's Yard Remedies
29 John Dalton Street,
Manchester, M2 6DS, UK
Email:
mailorder@nealsyardremedies.com

## HERBAL PRACTITIONER REGISTERS

**American Herbalists Guild**
Holds a list of approved herbal practitioners in the US.
AHG, 1931 Gaddis Road, Canton, GA 30115, USA
www.americanherbalistsguild.com
ahgoffice@earthlink.net

**College of Practitioners of Phytotherapy**
One of the major professional organisations for herbal medicine in the UK, it can provide a list of qualified phytotherapists.

**College of Phytotherapy,**
Rutherford Park, Marley lane, Battle, East Sussex TN33 OT7

**National Institute of Medical Herbalists**
Established in 1864, this is the main professional body for medical herbalists in the UK. It can provide details of training courses in herbal medicine and a directory of qualified practitioners.
56 Longbrook Street, Exeter, Devon EX4 6AH.
Telephone: 01392 426022
www.nimh.org.uk

# About the author

Peter Conway DipPhyt MNIMH MCPP CertEd is a practising medical herbalist, teacher and author. He is the editor of the *British Journal of Phytotherapy*, and is active in the fields of herbal education and regulation.

Peter practises at the Atman Clinic in Tunbridge Wells, Kent. He is a member of the National Institute of Medical Herbalists, and President of the College of Practitioners of Phytotherapy. His work has been featured in numerous publications, as well as on radio and TV. He lectures widely both in the UK and internationally.

# Other titles in the series

- Understanding Acupressure
- Understanding Acupuncture
- Understanding The Alexander Technique
- Understanding Aromatherapy
- Understanding Echinacea
- Understanding Evening Primrose
- Understanding Feng Shui
- Understanding Fish Oils
- Understanding Flower Remedies
- Understanding Garlic
- Understanding Head Massage
- Understanding Kinesiology
- Understanding Lavender
- Understanding Massage
- Understanding Pilates
- Understanding Reflexology
- Understanding Reiki
- Understanding Shiatsu
- Understanding Yoga

**For Morgaine**

I would like to acknowledge the work of my colleagues, particularly Michael McIntyre and Kerry Bone, in helping me to understand St. John's Wort.

The contents of this book are for information only and are not intended as a substitute for appropriate medical attention. The author and publishers admit no liability for any consequences arising from following any advice contained within this book. If you have any concerns about your health or medication, always consult your doctor.

The publishers wish to thank Rutland Biodynamics Ltd for help with the photography in this book.

**Line drawings: Viv Rainsbury**

First published 2003 by First Stone Publishing
4/5 The Marina, Harbour Road, Lydney, Gloucestershire, GL15 5ET

**ISBN 1-904439-020**

Printed and bound in Hong Kong through Printworks International Ltd.